MINIATURE STORIES *of the* SAINTS

BOOK THREE

BY REV. DANIEL A. LORD, S.J.

NIHIL OBSTAT: Arthur J. Scanlan S. T. D., Censor Librorum
IMPRIMATUR: Francis J. Spellman, D. D., Archbishop, New York

Published by:
William J. Hirten Co., Inc.
Brooklyn, New York

Saint Andrew
APOSTLE

Andrew was just a poor fisherman in Galilee. He had a brother whose name was Simon Peter.

One day he heard a great preacher, John the Baptist. He left his boats and fishing nets, and followed John.

And John said, "Someone is coming who is greater than I."

So when Jesus came, Andrew left John to follow Jesus. He ran and told Simon Peter. Peter went to Jesus too. Andrew and Peter both became Apostles.

Andrew was the Apostle who found the little boy with the loaves and fishes. Our dear Lord used these to feed thousands of people. That was a great miracle.

Jesus made Andrew one of His first Bishops.

"Go, teach everyone the Good News," Jesus said.

So after the Ascension of our Lord into heaven, Andrew went to Greece.

Some listened and became Christians.

But some hated Andrew because they hated Jesus.

So they nailed Andrew to a Cross. Andrew sang with joy because, like Jesus, he could die on the Cross.

He hung for two days on the Cross telling everyone about Jesus.

Then he went gloriously to heaven.

His Feast is November 30th.

Saint Augustine

BISHOP AND DOCTOR OF THE CHURCH

When Augustine was a young man, he was very clever and bright. His mother, Monica, was a good Catholic. But Augustine couldn't be bothered.

He didn't want to believe what Christ taught. He knew that what Christ taught was the truth, but he did not want to be good.

He led a very wicked life.

All this time, his mother, Monica, wept and prayed.

"Make my son a good man," she begged God. "Please make him believe and give up his sins."

One day Augustine heard that some of his friends had become Catholics. They were not nearly as bright as he was.

"How silly and foolish I am," he thought. "They will go to heaven. But I, to whom God gave such a fine mind, will lose my soul."

He ran to his mother and told her he wished to be good henceforth. She was very glad.

So he repented of his sins. He studied to be a priest.

He became a great Bishop. He did penance for his sins. And he wrote many wonderful books about God and the soul and goodness.

He fought untruth and he hated sin.

The young man who had been a sinner became the man who was a wise and holy saint.

His Feast is August 28th.

Saint Benedict

FATHER OF HOLY MONKS

The name Benedict means Blessed.

When Benedict was a boy, he realized that he was living in sad, not blessed days.

The world was full of savage and evil men. They made war on everybody. They destroyed beautiful buildings and burned wise books. They thought it was amusing to be destructive. They were very cruel.

Even the schoolboys were wicked and mean. They laughed at Benedict because he tried to be good.

So he ran away from the evil men and the sinful boys. He hid himself in a mountain near Subiaco.

He prayed. He studied. He talked with God. He asked God to make cruel men gentle and wicked little boys pure.

Soon many people heard about this wonderful young man. They hated war and evil men. So they ran up to the mountain and said to Benedict, "Let us stay with you."

Benedict built beautiful houses which are called monasteries. He dressed the good men as monks.

His sister, Saint Scholastica, dressed the women as nuns or sisters. She built convents.

In these the men and women prayed. They studied. They loved peace. They asked God to forgive sinners.

These men and women were the first Benedictines.

His Feast is July 11th.

Saint Christopher

THE CHRIST BEARER

Saint Christopher was a giant and very strong. He was a very brave soldier. "I will serve only the strongest men in the world," he said. So he fought in the army of a great, strong king.

But one day the soldier saw the king tremble and grow pale. The king was afraid of Satan. The thought of the Devil frightened him.

So Christopher, whose name was then Offero, went to serve the Devil. But soon he found that the Devil was afraid of someone too. Oh, he was very strong, but he was afraid of Jesus Christ.

"I will serve Jesus Christ," said Christopher.

So he went to a river where many travellers came. He carried them across on his strong shoulders. Some day, he thought, Jesus Christ might come that way.

Then one day a little Boy came to the river.

Christopher hoisted the Boy on his shoulders. He was very light. But as they crossed the river, He got heavier and heavier. "Who are You?" asked the giant. "I am Jesus Christ," said the Boy. "You looked for Me."

The giant was very happy. He became a Christian. His name became Christopher; that means, the man who carried Christ.

He is the patron saint of travellers. Especially he is the patron of those who travel in automobiles.

His traditional Feast is July 25th.

Saint Dominic

GREAT PREACHER

Dominic was a fine, brave young Spaniard.

He was a smart student, too. He also loved the poor, and sold even his clothes and books to give money to those who were hungry.

In those days, evil men hated Jesus Christ and the truth. They were called Albigenses. They destroyed homes. They burned churches. They killed Catholics, especially priests and nuns.

Bravely Dominic decided to gather an army to fight them. Only his was an army of peace. He gathered fine young men and dressed them in white.

"I shall call you the Order of Preachers," he said. Nowadays we call these fine priests the Dominicans.

Dominic and his priests went everywhere and taught people the truth about Jesus Christ and goodness.

He gathered pure young women and dressed them in white too.

"You will pray for sinners," he said. These were the first Dominican nuns.

To help him win his battle of peace, Mary, our Blessed Mother, gave him a powerful weapon.

It was her Rosary. With that, Dominic and his brave men and pure women overcame the enemies of Christ and His Church.

His traditional Feast is August 4th.

Saint Edward
THE CONFESSOR

Edward was one of the greatest Kings of England. He was called the Confessor, because he confessed his belief in Jesus Christ. He admitted proudly that he was a Catholic. He ruled his Kingdom as Christ wanted it ruled.

Edward never expected to be king. Indeed, when he was very young, bad men drove him away from England. But the good people remembered him. They knew he would be a fine king.

So when he was forty years old, they brought him back. "Be our king!" they cried. And he accepted.

He was a very good king. He loved the poor. He spent his money to make them happy.

He was never proud. Instead of sitting on a throne, he walked the streets, talking with people, asking them their troubles, helping them to be happy.

He married a very good queen. They lived pure lives. People said, "There is a perfect husband and wife."

Often sick people came to him. He touched them and they were cured. All his laws were good. They helped make his people happy.

He was king for twenty four years. There were no wars. The country grew rich and gay.

Before he died, he built the Westminster Abbey.

His Feast is October 13th.

Saint Gregory

THE POPE

Young Gregory's father was very rich.

When his father died, Gregory gave all the money he inherited to the poor. Then he went to a monastery and became a monk. He prayed. He studied hard.

The Pope of those days heard about this bright young man. He called Gregory to Rome. He made him a Deacon. He sent him on important errands to kings and generals.

One day in the market place, Gregory saw some slaves. They told him they were Angles.

"You should be Angels," he said.

English boys were called Angles in those days. Gregory knew they did not believe in Jesus. You see, he hoped they would be Catholics. When the Pope died, the people made Gregory the Pope.

He remembered the English boys. So he sent Saint Augustine to England to tell them about Jesus and to make them Catholics. He sent holy priests to convert the Spanish and the French. Wicked men came rushing into Italy to destroy it.

He told them about Jesus, and they became Catholics too. He wrote great books which are still read.

He taught people how to sing in Church. We still call these songs the Gregorian Chants.

He was one of the greatest Popes that ever lived.

His traditional Feast is March 12th.

Saint Ignatius

A MARTYR AND A JESUIT

There are two great saints named Ignatius.

One was the Bishop of Antioch. Saint John the Apostle taught him to know and love Jesus.

The Blessed Sacrament was very dear to his heart. He was always teaching people that Jesus gave them His flesh to eat and His blood to drink.

The Roman Emperor was angry because Ignatius would not call him a god. So he dragged him to Rome.

"Let the lions devour him!" the Emperor ordered.

Ignatius was glad to die for the truth.

Jesus had given His flesh in Holy Communion for him.

So he gave his flesh to the lions for love of Jesus.

The other saint who was named Ignatius was a brave soldier and was called Saint Ignatius of Loyola.

One day he was wounded badly in battle. When he was getting well, he read the Lives of the Saints.

"What they did, I can do!" he thought. And he became the brave soldier of Christ.

So he established a new Society of Priests and Brothers. He called it the Society of Jesus.

The Feast of St. Ignatius of Antioch is February 1st.

The Feast of St. Ignatius of Loyola is July 31st.

Saint Jerome

WHO LOVED THE BIBLE

Saint Jerome was one of the wisest men that ever lived. But at first he was not wise at all.

He was just clever. He knew a great deal. And he loved to show off. He liked to have people think him bright. He said things that sounded smart, even if they were not true.

But one day Christ spoke to his heart. Then Jerome knew that the truth of Christ was the important truth.

He ran away to the desert. He lived in a cave. He prayed. He studied a lot. He read the Gospels over and over again. He became a truly wise man.

"Come back to Rome," the Pope said at last.

So Jerome obeyed. He knew the Gospels better than anyone in the world. He prepared the Bible so that everyone could read it.

But he wanted to return to the land where our Lord had lived.

So he left Rome and went to Bethlehem.

He wrote beautiful letters to people all over the world. In these letters he told them all about Jesus and His truth.

He wrote clear explanations of the Gospels.

He prayed to God. And God taught him everything he wanted to know.

All this he taught to others.

His Feast is September 30th.

Saint Stanislaus Kostka
THE BOY SAINT

Stanislaus Kostka was a young Polish nobleman. His father was a rich man. So Stanislaus was brought up in the court.

Sometimes, men sitting at dinner said nasty things. When they did, little Stanislaus blushed. It made him ill to hear men say dirty and unpleasant things.

He went away to school with his big brother. But his big brother was a bully. He treated Stanislaus badly. So there was nothing to do but run away.

He did. His brother followed him with fast horses. But when they passed Stanislaus on the road, God did not let the brother see the runaway.

On that journey he came to an empty church. Oh, how he wished he could go to Holy Communion! But there was no priest. How could he receive? God took care of that. Angels brought Holy Communion to the boy. He walked all the way from Vienna to Rome.

He begged his food. The Blessed Virgin appeared to him and told him she would take care of him.

He became a Jesuit novice. From the start he showed he was a saint. He loved to pray. He was very pure.

But Mary, his Mother and ours, came for him on the Feast of the Assumption and took him with her to heaven.

His traditional Feast is November 13th.

Saint Leo the Great
THE POPE

The name Leo means the Lion.

And Saint Leo, the Pope, was a lion in bravery.

The Vandals and Huns, two terrible races, were fighting the Christians of Europe.

Besides this, evil men were teaching people lies about Jesus. They were saying what was not true and getting the people confused. Leo became Pope. He had been a smart and wise young man.

Now he had to be a brave and very wise Pope.

First he went everywhere teaching the truth about our dear Lord. He called together all the wise priests and bishops of the Church. This was the great Council of Chalcedon.

They talked and studied and listened.

And they went home to teach their people the truth. So people did not believe the evil men any more when they lied about the Savior.

But the Vandals and Huns kept coming. They burned cities. They murdered people everywhere.

All alone, without weapons, Leo went out to meet them.

Their leader Attila was called the Awful Scourge.

But when he saw Leo he ordered his armies to cease fighting. Instead of destroying Rome, they turned and went away. The Pope had saved Europe.

His traditional Feast is April 11th.

Saint Matthew

WRITER OF THE GOSPEL

Once upon a time there was a tax gatherer named Levi.

The Jews did not like him. He took their tax money and gave it to the Romans. But Levi was not a bad man. He only did what he thought was his duty.

One day Jesus saw him. He saw good in him that others did not see. "Come and follow Me!" Jesus said quietly to the tax gatherer.

Levi looked up in surprise. He had never seen such a wonderful Man before. Why, it would be the greatest honor to be one of His followers!

Instantly he got up. He left his table with all the money on it. He went after our Lord. And Jesus made him one of His twelve Apostles.

He changed his name to Matthew. He wrote the wonderful Gospel According to Saint Matthew.

He saw all that Jesus did. He heard all that Jesus said. He walked with Him and grew to love Him more and more.

To make sure that the world would never forget Jesus, Matthew wrote all this down in his beautiful Gospel. Gospel, you know, means Good News.

He died a blessed martyr.

With Saint Mark, Saint Luke and Saint John, he is one of the Four Evangelists.

His Feast is September 21st.

Saint Philip Neri

THE CHEERFUL SAINT

When Philip Neri was a young boy he lived in Rome. He had a terrible temper. He was afraid that some day he would flare up and hurt some one badly.

So he set himself to cure his temper.

He determined always to be cheerful. He learned to smile all the time. He loved to laugh. He was always pleasant. People loved just to see him and have him speak to them. Especially he loved the Holy Spirit.

Indeed, once the Holy Spirit was seen to come down upon the young Philip. He shone with the light of the Third Person of the Trinity.

Philip became a priest. He started a little church in which he gathered friends. They prayed together. They sang together. He said Mass for them. They walked in happy processions through the streets. They crowned the statue of Our Lady.

The little church was called the Oratory. That means, it was a lovely place to pray. People came to him sad. He sent them away happy. They came with their sins. He sent them away pure in soul.

Children followed him. Sinners saw how lovely it is not to sin. He made evil men love God. He taught everyone the happiness of goodness.

They called him the Apostle of Rome.

His Feast is May 26th.

Saint Louis

THE KING OF FRANCE

Louis was a fine, strong, pure boy. His mother taught him to hate sin. Her name was Blanche.

"I love you, my son," she said; "but I would rather see you dead than have you commit one mortal sin."

He remembered this all his life. He was made King of France. He determined to be a good and generous king. So he established great schools.

He made wise laws. He gave money freely to the poor. He stopped evil men who were teaching lies to the people. Each day he found time to hear two Masses. He prayed far into the night.

In those days, the Moslems hated Christians. They were trying to destroy the Christian countries. They had great armies. They sailed powerful fleets. It looked as if they would win.

But Louis made sure they would not.

He gathered a great army and marched out to fight them. He was so brave and fine that the Moslems respected him. Some of them asked him to be their king.

Yet God did not wish him to win with the sword. He really seemed to lose that war. Only he didn't. The Moslems never conquered Christian lands. Other brave men fought as King Louis had done.

Europe was saved for Christ.

His Feast is August 25th.

Saint Luke

THE EVANGELIST

Saint Luke studied medicine when he was a young man and became a great doctor.

He was also a skillful painter.

One day he heard about Jesus Christ. He knew that Jesus was the Great Physician. He was sure that Jesus was the God who had made all the beautiful world.

So Saint Luke followed Jesus as His disciple.

He was very close to Saint Paul and travelled with him. He was a clever writer. So he wrote down all that the Apostles did.

This book we call the Acts of the Apostles.

Then he went to see Our Lady. He asked her all about the Baby Jesus. He wrote what she told him in the Gospel According to Saint Luke.

He asked the other Apostles what they knew about Jesus, and their stories are told in his Gospel.

He travelled with Saint Paul all over the world.

He told people that although he could heal their bodies, only Jesus could heal their souls.

He painted a lovely picture of the Blessed Virgin.

We still have copies of it.

In the end, the pagans of Greece killed him because they hated Jesus.

His Feast is October 18th.

INRI

Saint Robert

THE MONK

Robert was a young monk who lived in England.

He heard that a group of holy young men wanted to love God very much. They wanted to be especially good to sinners. So he left his comfortable home and joined them. Soon other brave young men came. Together they built a beautiful monastery.

There the poor could come for food. England had few hotels in those days. So travellers could stay over night in Robert's monastery. He gathered boys and girls to teach them about Jesus. He welcomed the sick and took care of them in his hospital.

He never ate until the poor were fed. He gave away his own clothes. He sat up all night long to care for the sick. Once, as he was sitting at dinner, a friend gave him bread sweetened with honey.

But through the window, he saw a poor man. He picked up the bread and honey, placed it on a plate, and carried it to the poor man.

Next day, as he sat at dinner, the plate appeared in the air. It was bright and shining like gold. Then the monks knew that the poor man to whom Robert had given the bread and honey was Christ Himself.

When Robert died, his soul, like a bright ball of fire, went straight up into heaven. The monks heard God's voice saying, "Enter into heaven!"

His Feast is June 7th.

Saint Sebastian

THE SOLDIER

Sebastian was a captain in the Roman army, a fine officer and a brave soldier.

One day he heard about Jesus Christ and said, "He is the one I want to follow." So from that day he loved Christ and fought bravely for Him.

One day his two brothers were arrested. "You are Christians, and you must die," said the judge.

They were only boys, and they were afraid. But Sebastian comforted them, saying, "Don't be afraid. We shall all be martyrs. It is glorious to die for Christ."

The Mayor of Rome did not believe in Jesus Christ. He heard about Sebastian and sent for the young soldier. "Tell me about Jesus," he ordered. And Sebastian talked so beautifully that the Mayor became a Christian too. This made the people who hated Jesus very angry. They began to kill the Christians.

Many of the Christians fled from Rome. Although Sebastian helped them escape he refused to leave.

So the Romans arrested Sebastian. They tied him to a stake. Soldiers shot at him with bows and arrows.

They left him for dead. But Sebastian was not dead. He was still alive and he went to the judge who had ordered him shot. "Please believe in Jesus," he begged. But instead they beat him to death with clubs.

His traditional Feast is January 20th.

Saint Stephen

THE FIRST MARTYR

Stephen loved Jesus very much. He worked hard for the poor. He told everyone that Christ was their Savior.

So many people followed him. They listened while he spoke. For his eyes were bright with love for Jesus. And he spoke beautifully of what Jesus had taught and done.

One day the enemies of Jesus said, "We must stop this man. We killed Jesus. But this Stephen still makes others believe in Jesus. We must kill him too."

First they ordered him to stop preaching. He laughed. He could not stop talking about the Savior he loved. So they caught him. They dragged him outside the city.

He stood facing them, this fine young man.

He loved them because Jesus had died for their sakes. He hoped he could make them all Christians.

So he told them about Jesus. He reminded them that Jesus was the very Savior they had hoped to see. He told them that Jesus was not dead but had ascended into heaven.

Angrily, they picked up rocks. They flung them at Stephen. He fell dead. But first he saw Jesus coming to take him.

He was the first martyr.

His Feast is December 26th.

Saint Francis Xavier

THE MISSIONARY

Saint Francis Xavier went to the University of Paris.

He was a champion runner. He was a great athlete. But he was a very clever student, too.

In class, he was the leader. He learned easily. He studied hard.

"I want to be a great professor," he said. "I want to know all there is to know. I want people to listen when I talk. I want to write wonderful books."

Then he met Saint Ignatius Loyola.

"What good will it do you," Ignatius asked him, "if you win the whole world and then lose your soul?"

Francis thought this over. He decided he could win the world and at the same time save his soul. So he became a friend of Saint Ignatius. He became a Jesuit.

"Send me out," he said, "and I will win the world for our dear Lord."

So Ignatius sent him out as a missionary.

He went to India. He told people there about Jesus.

He went to Japan. The pagans listened. Many of them too became Catholics.

Then he wanted to go to China. Instead, he died on a little island just off the coast of China.

But he had converted thousands and thousands.

He was the greatest missionary since the days of the Apostles.

His Feast is December 3rd.

CONTENTS

BOOK THREE

Printed in Korea